How to Grow Your Veterinary Practice by Working *Smarter* Not Harder

How to Grow Your Veterinary Practice by Working *Smarter* Not Harder.

Copyright © 2015

Table of Contents

$* * *$

Introduction

* * *

"Build your own dreams, or someone else will hire you to build theirs." —Farrah Gray

In a veterinary practice, no day is the same because each animal patient brings a new challenge and reward. The workweek also won't fall under the standard of forty hours, especially if the practice already handles many clients. Animal emergencies can happen any time, including nights, weekends and holidays. The US Bureau of Labor Statistics show that one in three veterinarians worked more than fifty hours per week in 2012.

Being a vet can be a very gratifying career. You have the gift of healing companions, which many people consider to be part of their family. But you'll agree that it also comes with a lot of challenges, especially if you are in solo practice and have your own clinic.

If you look at your day-to-day activity and workload, are you the one doing most of the work in your clinic? When was the last time you took a real vacation? Have you ever asked your assistant to do something, yet ended up doing the task yourself? How many of these tasks are *reactive* (to your status quo) rather than *proactive* (to prepare your business for growth)?

These are just a few of the questions you'll want to ask yourself as you close in on achieving the work-life balance that you've always wanted. As a solo practitioner, it is common to feel the need to micromanage everything. However, you need to check whether you are growing your business in a way that helps you create the life you've always dreamed about living, or if it's sapping all your energy and time, and feels more like a ball and chain around your leg.

As a professional, you know how to do your job very well. So you decided to open your own clinic and you do your job — what you were trained to do — work as a vet. But here's the most common mistake made by vets in solo practice. They only see it as a *job*, and fail to see it as a *business*.

That's a really big difference.

Here's the litmus test to determine whether you're thinking about your clinic as a job or as a business: if you spend most of your time caught up in the day-to-day operations of running your clinic — making farm calls, handling emergency situations, battling mounds of paperwork, leaving messages for people who don't readily return your calls — then you're thinking of your clinic as a job.

Familiar with the saying that the word "job" is an acronym for *Just Over Broke?* If this hits a little close to home for you, if this is the way that you've been thinking and operating, then please know that it's not your fault. It's simply because no one has ever taught you any differently.

Jeff had a horrible feeling the dog
needed his worming tablets again.

If, however, you're someone who spends time thinking about the direction in which you want your practice to go — and taking action to make that a reality — then you're thinking like a true *business* owner.

Regardless of where you are right now with building your practice, I want you to think of it as *the vehicle to getting what you really want in life.* You want to work only twenty hours a week, while making more money than you make right now? It's time to make it happen. You want to take six weeks off a year on vacation, to spend with your family? Yes, it *is* possible — just not at this precise moment, because you don't have your business set up in a way that supports this yet. *It's important to remember that **you** are in the driver's seat. You simply have to turn the steering wheel towards the right goal.*

When I opened my first business, I confess that (far too often) my days were focused on doing things that could very well have been done by someone else. It was just so easy to get caught up in that mess — of working "in" the business instead of "on" the business.

My promise to you is simple. In this book, I'm going to share with you a step-by-step plan to help you achieve a level of clarity for your business that will bring you the success and lifestyle that you want. I'm going to show you how to break the limits of your mindset by refocusing on the unlimited opportunities that are out there. And I'm going to show you some simple techniques to help you make a few small changes in your practice that can deliver astonishing returns. You've heard the saying, "Little hinges swing big doors."

This book is all about helping you identify those "little hinges" in your practice, to help you get the biggest results.

Here's how I've broken things down:

In Chapter 1, I'm going to talk about what I call the Disconnect between the *business* and the veterinary *profession*. I'm going to help you look a little deeper into your practice and accurately diagnose the level of disconnect that you currently have.

Then, in Chapter 2, we'll discuss the Transformational Experience Ladder. When we start a business of our own, it's just like a ladder. We start from the bottom and (hopefully) keep moving upwards. Those folks who keep thinking of their business as a job, unfortunately, get stuck on the first rung. (And that's where the majority of small business owners end up — through no fault of their own. They have no clue that there are all these other steps available to them!) I will show you how to get from being simply the *manager* to becoming an *entrepreneur* and then a *leader*.

Chapter 3 illustrates something I call the Strategic Turning Point. This is about finding the right tools, and thinking about ways to bring your practice to the next level, which will help you attract more clients and increase your revenue.

In Chapter 4, I'm going to talk about Productivity Levers. These are the two things that you need to learn how to "re-manage" — to be able to maximize your productivity and efficiency. I will also discuss the actions you should take to get the best return for the time and money that you've invested.

In Chapter 5, we're going to discuss what it takes to ignite your Third Factor. This is where you determine how you will differentiate *your* practice from the rest, and how you create value for your clients. Once you've ignited your Third Factor, you don't ever have to worry about your competition — ever again. This was a major turning point for me in my business, and it enabled me to build a thriving, multi-million dollar business in a tiny town in Alberta with major chain store competitors within easy driving distance (more about that later).

Chapter 6 is where I'll be sharing with you some of the more costly mistakes I've made myself. These aren't things any of us usually care to re-live, much less recount to others! But my hope is that you will be able to avoid "reinventing the wheel" — and instead learn from my experience!

Last, Chapter 7 will discuss the Magic of Making Things Happen. A plan is just a plan, unless you *do* it. The information here will help you focus on doing just a few things really well to start seeing results.

As a business coach, I've used the following analogy with my vet clients many times. Imagine for a minute that you're a honeybee, living in a beehive. Now, as a honeybee, you have an important choice to make. You can choose to be a worker bee and do all the hard physical labour — flying around from flower to flower, travelling miles every day and carting back to the hive as many sacks of pollen as you can, and helping to build the colony. Or you can choose to be the queen bee, the one I call the "Super Bee" — the one in charge — doing none (or very little) of the physical labour yourself, but instead providing the leadership skills that enable *the rest of the hive* to build the colony. Acting as the *manager* of your practice does not equate to being the Super Bee, because as manager, you're not at the top of the ladder. You can still go higher than that.

Lorraine working smart — taking a very rejuvenating free day

I want my clients to think of themselves as the Super Bee in their business, to free themselves up from doing the mundane tasks of running a business, and working just on those areas they love the most. I hope that this is what you want, too — if it is, please read on!

The Lesson of the Hobbled Horse

I grew up on a farm in Alberta. Every spring, the boys in our family — my dad, my brother and I — would go camping with our horses. Usually we would bring with us a couple of new horses that hadn't had many hours under the saddle — it always made life interesting! My dad was the ringleader and the one who called all the shots, my brother was the cowboy who had a special way of communicating with the horses, and as for me — I was the one who inevitably ended up in the saddle of the green horses, sometimes holding on for dear life!

Once we got to our campsite, the first thing we'd need to do was hobble the horses. (For those in Small Animal practice who may not have experience with horses, a "hobble" is simply a restraint that keeps the horse from wandering when there's nothing readily available to tie it up to.) That way we knew when we woke up, the horses (hopefully) wouldn't be too far away and it wouldn't be a long walk home!

Hobbling one of the green horses was always an interesting event. Inevitably, one of four things would happen to a horse that was being hobbled for the first time:

8

1. The horse would freeze the first second he felt the hobbles around his legs, and would remain virtually glued to the same spot all night long, without moving.
2. The horse would turn out to be what we called "a shuffler". These horses learned really quickly to shuffle so they could walk as fast as possible despite their legs being hobbled.
3. It thought its life was about to end, began to panic, and became a "jumper" — jumping around all over the place like a cat on a hot tin roof. Of course, this never lasted too long, because it ended up just tiring out.
4. And then there was the "everything" hobbled horse, doing a combination of all three. It figured out pretty quickly that if it combined all three techniques, it could conserve its energy and cover the most ground possible in the shortest amount of time. These were the horses we had to put a bell on because they covered so much ground!

This was always a memorable experience — it's interesting to see how horses react to new situations. Human behavior is not that different. When we experience something new — or we feel threatened — how often do we freeze, shuffle or jump, or do all three? As someone who owns a business, or who recently started one, which one are you? As you're asking that of yourself, let me relate a bit about myself, and how I came to my own answer to that question. I think it's important for you to decide for yourself the kind of person I am, and whether I'm qualified to help you create an "auto-pilot" vet practice the way I've created an "auto-pilot" in my own business.

I am not a veterinarian. I've never been one, and have no intention of becoming one. I have, however, worked with hundreds of vets over the years — and I think it's fair to say that I understand the challenges you face in your business — inside out. (You don't have to just take my word for it, though. Look over what other vets have had to say about me, at the end of this book.)

Neither am I one of those business coaches who "coach" but have very little "in-the-trenches" experience of running their own business — that is not me. In fact, nothing could be further from the truth.

I know exactly what it's like to experience the thrill of opening your own business, the stress of keeping it running, working all hours of the day and night, tackling staff problems, client problems, vendor problems — I know as well as you do that the list of challenges is long. And I know what it's like to work in a fiercely competitive industry — there are new, hungry graduates opening up private practices all over the place, smaller vet practices are consolidating and forming bigger practices so they can offer cheaper pricing, and who knows but the Big Box Stores will be offering veterinary care right next to the optometrist and pharmacy soon. You're likely working back-breaking hours already, hardly ever getting a chance to take even a weekend (much less a whole weekend!) off. Your phone beeps all hours of the day and night, cutting into your precious family time and rendering any plans you might make disjointed and stressful — not to mention the fact you arrive back at work on Monday exhausted, rather than refreshed...

Hiking with our kids on our anniversary weekend

These problems are not unique to vets. *But they are unique to business owners.* Regardless whether you're a home-office accountant, or own the corner store, or you've taken your garage-startup to billions of dollars in revenue (like Steve Jobs did), the challenges of successfully running a business — *and not have it run you* — are the same for us all.

An Entrepreneurial Start

I got my first job when I was twelve years old, delivering the daily newspaper. I had to order the paper and then deliver it to customers. It was my first entrepreneurial experience.

11

Every time I walked by houses, I thought, "Why aren't they getting papers from me?" So, I made it a goal that every time I delivered papers, I would knock on two or three doors to get new customers. Also, since Friday was the day a lot people wanted to read newspapers, I'd have two extra papers that I'd sell on the main street. If I was lucky, I could sell them at twelve cents each. I ended up with the biggest paper route in town.

From there, I went on to work in a men's clothing store, selling suits and dress clothes. One of the owners of the store wanted to open a new branch in another town, and he asked me to come with him. For me, it was the best education I could ever have had, because he delegated a lot of the duties to me *and he paid me for it*. They had a sporting goods department, and he assigned me to manage it. I did all the buying and promoting for that department.

I went to college after that, and took up business administration. I also played hockey. Lorraine, my high school sweetheart (who would become my wife), was working at university to get her Bachelor's of Science. I ended up working again in the men's clothing store because I was learning a lot from the owner — the real world application of the things I had learned in the classroom. When Lorraine graduated, she worked for three months in the same town.

We didn't stay there for long, though, because my dad asked Lorraine to come work for him in his small pharmacy in our hometown of Barrhead, Alberta. He also knew that I was looking for something besides the men's clothing business

— I'd been doing that a long time and didn't find it much of a challenge anymore. He asked me to step in and run the business.

So Lorraine and I jumped in — with both feet, working day and night. We were there first thing in the morning to open the doors and greet customers, and we were there last thing at night to lock everything up and get things ready for the next day. We were also on call twenty-four hours a day. Those early years were definitely a hard grind — our home phone rang at all hours — there were no pagers or cell phones back then — interrupting our evenings and waking up the kids.

At that point we had a total of seven people working for us — and neither Lorraine nor I had any experience in managing staff, so it became a trial by fire. We quickly had to learn how to hire, train, develop and sometimes fire staff in relatively quick succession. At one point, our store got robbed. Somebody threw a crowbar through the window, robbed our drug cabinet and took off with armloads of cigarettes. So for a time, we were actually sleeping in the store. Money was tight. We were barely making ends meet and Lorraine was still paying off her substantial college loan.

Feeling excited yet about our prospects for success? But wait, there's more! Not only are we *not* the only pharmacy in town (there are, in fact, *five* direct competitors in our little town), but we also happen to be within very easy driving distance from several Big Box chain stores that offer heavily discounted medications (far cheaper than we do).

In the beginning I was exhausted, working long hours, and I certainly could not afford to take a vacation. I had a young family, and I realized that if I kept running the business the way I had been, I was either going to burn out or collapse — or both. So, out of *sheer desperation*, I started making changes— some small, some drastic — and not all at once, but I began to steadily make improvements to the way I ran things. Today, my pharmacy is a multi-million dollar business — one of the most successful privately owned pharmacies in North America — and even better, it runs just as well without me as it does with me there.

I know that because, unfortunately, we've had to truly test the auto-pilot capabilities of our business. I say "unfortunately" because it wasn't due to our going on some amazing worldwide trip, or deciding to hang up hammocks and take a quarter of the year off sipping margaritas in the sun. No, my wife Lorraine was diagnosed with cancer, which instantly turned our entire world upside down. She also happens to be the head pharmacist, so on a regular day, the two of us are usually working in and on our business. But with her cancer diagnosis and subsequent surgery and treatment, though I occasionally worked in the business an hour or two here or there, the business had to practically run itself over the next three months. We explained the situation to key members of our staff, handed the reins over to them, and knew that we wouldn't come back to a disaster on our hands. Over this period we also hired new staff, which proved that our hiring processes were robust and didn't require our involvement.

Our staff were amazing. They all stepped up, and the business continued chugging along just fine without us. In fact, the revenue during the time when we worked in the business and the time we weren't there was *virtually the same!*

Our wonderful staff

Though we all hope and pray that something like this will never happen in our lives or the lives of the people we love, there are two important lessons here to take away:

1. Count your blessings, and do everything you can to make all your days with your loved ones the best they can possibly be.
2. All the work, time and energy you put into your business should be focused towards the goal of being free to leave it behind when you want, or need, to!

Despite our challenges, our many, many mistakes and the amount of competition we faced, little by little, we've been able to grow the business, and have taken it through many different levels. We have expanded the size of our store to twice its original size. We have also grown our number of employees to twenty-one, and two of them are part of the original four employees. We still operate night and day and our sales grow exponentially year after year, even though Barrhead is only a small town.

As you read through this book, you will hear more of my personal stories, and also stories from my vet clients, people just like you. You will hear how they used to run their operations, the challenges that they've experienced, and how — by tweaking some of the "little hinges" in their businesses — they've been able to swing some big doors.

My ultimate goal for you is to be able to go on a vacation, leave your business behind — and when you come back, to find it in the same condition as the day you left it. This book will show you how to enjoy your professional business like never before. The take away is this: learn how to set up your business so it runs smoothly on its own, determine the strategies you need to grow your business, create that one factor that makes you different, and then… take action!

Ready? I am if you are. Let's get started.

Chapter 1 — The Disconnect Between the Business and the Profession

* * *

"Your time is limited, so don't waste it living someone else's life." —Steve Jobs

After twenty eight years of working alongside veterinary professionals who also own their clinics, I have discovered that there is a fundamental disconnect between the *profession* that you're practicing and the *business* that you're running.

Does this sound like your day? Not enough time. A lack of control. Constant worry over customers and employees. Late night or weekend emergencies. Wishing you could delegate some of the necessary tasks, but hesitant to actually let go the reins.

You're not alone. Many professionals who own their business end up feeling like they've become slaves to that business. The constant worrying about the operating side of it makes them wonder if they'd be better off as just a worker bee for someone else, and let *that* person have the headache!

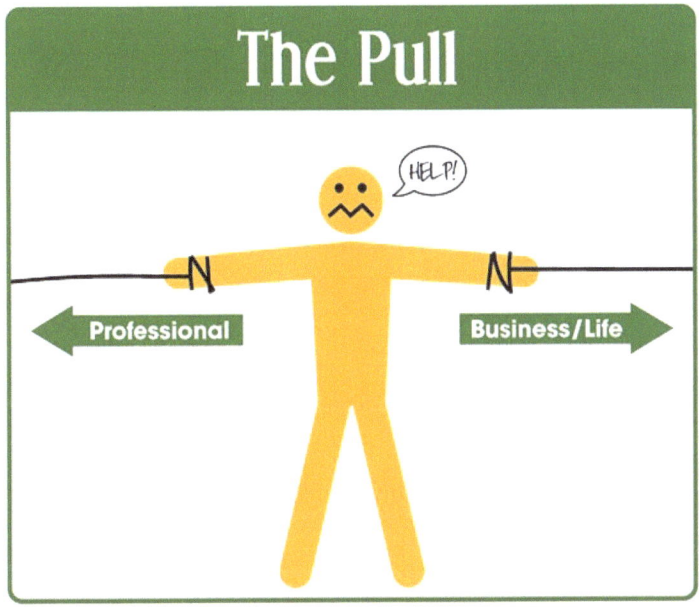

But you decided to run your own business for good reasons — more control, and more freedom of choice. So, as you would in your profession, we're going to examine this very important patient: the business side of your practice.

On one side, you have your profession as a veterinarian, and on the other side you have the business. On one side, there's taking care of your patients and trying your best to cure the animals. On the other side, there's getting income, paying the overhead and hoping there's some left over for you and your family.

Somewhere between these two sides there's a gap, or disconnect.

You are reading this book because you know there's something lacking in your solo practice. And the first thing you need to do, before taking any action, is to diagnose where you are right now in your business.

After we conduct the diagnostics of this disconnect, we are going to create a strategic plan or remedy for your patient, your business, and then we are going to put that plan into action.

At the start of every workshop that I do, I ask participants how much time they spend in a week working towards the things that will make their business the kind of business they want it to be. I call this doing the Super Bee work. And so they write down a number, usually as a percentage, on their notepads.

And then I tell them to discard accounting or financial activity. Their number becomes smaller. Honestly, most of them end up with a number of only two to five percent. This is the true amount of time they spend really concentrating on what it is that they want from their business and how to get it — the strategic planning.

©Scott Hilburn/Distributed by Universal Uclick via CartoonStock.com

Running a business can be chaotic. It's so easy to get sucked into the day-to-day operations because it is what you think is demanded from you. But when you spend time on strategic planning, you're saying, "I'm ready to take this business to the next level." The good thing about being an entrepreneur is that you have control of things. However, control can just be an illusion if you don't have a plan in mind.

Let me give you an example. When you have a computer problem, it can waste a lot of your time. The computer puts you in "reactive" mode as you troubleshoot and try to fix it. It's frustrating, because it's not doing what you want it to do for you. This is what running a business with a disconnect is like. What you need is to get out of that *reactive* mode and put yourself in *proactive* mode.

Constantly remind yourself why you're doing what you do. As entrepreneurial guru Dan Kennedy says: "You're here today to cross the swamp, not to fight the alligators."

For your practice to be successful, you first need to work on the disconnect between your profession and your business. I have developed a five-step process that will help you diagnose and address this problem, which this book will walk you through.

1. Leverage your Transformation Ladder.
2. Discover your Strategic Turning Point.
3. Manage the Productivity Levers of your business.
4. Ignite your Third Factor.
5. Make it all happen.

In the next chapter, we're going to talk about the first step, the Transformation Ladder, and how to position yourself in your business. This is the first step to really making things happen the way *you* want them to happen, to connecting the profession you love with the business you've always dreamed could be possible.

Chapter 2 — The Transformational Experience Ladder: From Job to Small Business to Manager to Leader

* * *

"You can never cross the ocean until you have the courage to lose sight of the shore." —Christopher Columbus

N ow I want to talk about the Transformational Experience Ladder. This is the professional or career experience that everybody climbs up. We *all* go through this. We all hit ceilings at every step, and when we hit those ceilings, we have to crash through them to go up to the next level.

It starts, of course, down at the bottom. This is where you received your license to become a veterinarian. So, now you're a professional and you have a job. And when you're first starting out, you're mentored by another vet who is older and more experienced than you are. During that mentorship period, you learn the ropes and you get confident. And then you hit your first ceiling.

And as we hit that ceiling, we say, "Well, the next step for me, naturally, is to go out and start a business." So you start a business. And from this stage, you are now an entrepreneur.

Then what happens is you do what you know best, which is your job, your profession, and you manage that job. And then your business grows, and you hit another ceiling. You've reached the point where your business no longer grows. So, to increase your income, you increase your number of clients. Sound familiar?

Eventually, then, you feel like you're becoming a slave to your business. It is beginning to wear on you. And then the business doesn't seem to grow, no matter what you do. You start buying new equipment, a fancy computer system. You keep longer hours. But you realize that the more work you input, the more output is expected from you. The more capital you add in, the more debt you have to pay. There's more and more to *manage*. For most people, this is where they end up. They create a whole bunch of headaches, the business gets more complicated, and at the end of the day, they have little to show for it but a lot more stress.

We need to transform you into what I call Position A. This is the position from which you lead an organization. You don't need to be a *manager*, you need to be a *leader*. You need to lead your group of people so that your business will be generating income for you, whether you're there or not.

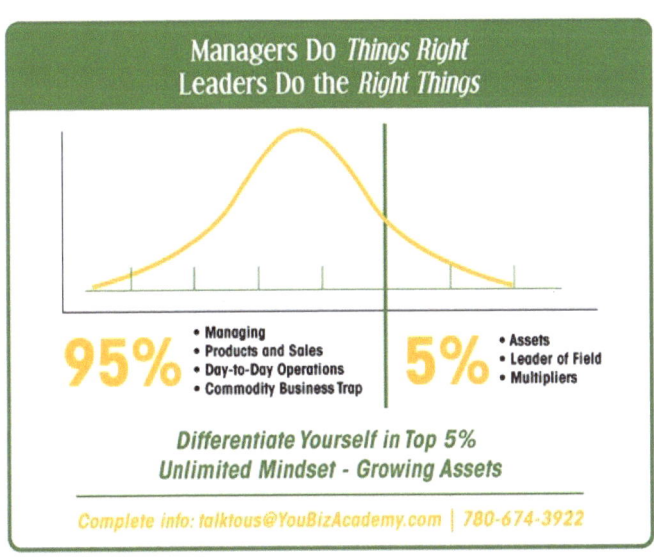

As a Position A leader, you have the same amount of time as a person who is below you on the Transformation Ladder, but you use it more wisely. You also have the same finances, only you start leveraging them and you start spending them more effectively.

Some practitioners hire another vet when they are on vacation. You might bring that person in, but that person is not going to give the same service as you do. Why is that? Precisely because this is a different vet who does not know how you work. They don't approach their patients in the same way you do — and don't necessarily invest the time to build real relationships with them either.

The key to this is being able to standardize your patients' experience when they come to your clinic. This is the first step to moving up your ladder. A substitute vet becomes a *representative* of your practice. He or she should be able to give the same experience as you do, even though it's not you delivering the service.

The second thing you need to do in your transformation process is to use your creativity. Creativity, simply put, is knowing your clients — how to help them understand where they want to be, and how to help them get there. You don't necessarily have to be good at this yourself. You surround yourself with the right people, with the right plan, and things start to grow. That's *really* where the fun begins.

The third step is to build the right relationships. I don't just mean with your clients, though, obviously, that's extremely important. But it should also be with the members of your team: the people working in your clinic, your outsourced accountant, your financial advisor, a coach you partner with. It should be with people in your community, and networking with other veterinarians. It should always be with your family. We all have the potential to give and receive the best, in our relationships — to help make each other better, and to become better ourselves.

In our company, we like to have team meetings offsite. You learn so much about each other when you're together out of "the office" — what their aspirations are, what they want from their work — and the relationships we've built doing this over the years are very special. My kids, now adults, to this day get big hugs every time they visit the store.

Offsite weekend with key leaders of our company and their spouses — great memories and very productive

All these steps will help you move into Position A. This is what we call the Transformational Experience. Our role is to become industry transformational experience leaders by helping people or customers get from one point to another. This is the best way to turn your business into a valuable business.

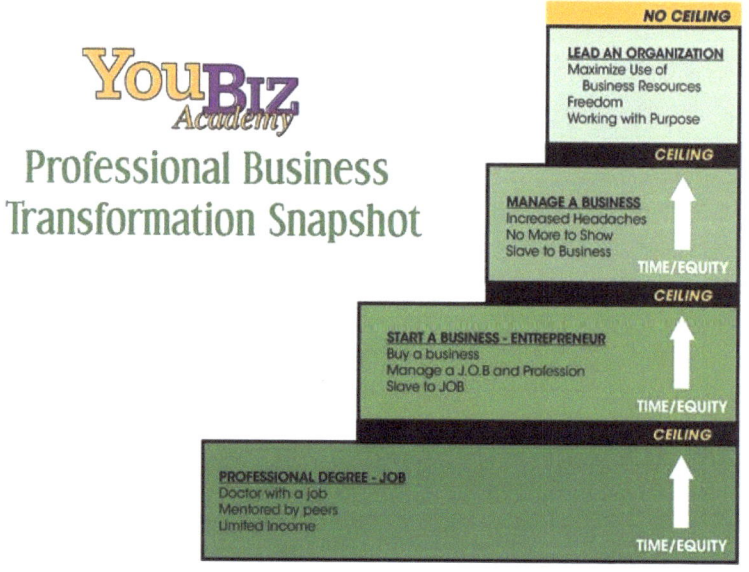

This is the ultimate level that you want to reach. You're not just a Doctor of Veterinary Medicine, you are also an executive business owner. This ties into a couple things we're going to talk about in a bit: leveraging your return-on-equity and your return-on-energy. As your organization grows, the headaches might grow, but you are more effective with the energy that you put into it, and more effective with your assets or equity.

I'll share with you a couple stories about my vet clients. One was a "solopreneur" — a solo entrepreneur. She took all the calls, did all the billing, and worked out of a truck. She heard me at a one-day business workshop at which I was a guest speaker. The part that she gravitated to at that time was that she was a worker bee in her own hive. She knew she needed to change that.

So she hired an assistant. After following the steps I showed her, her business grew like crazy; she couldn't keep up with it. Now she has another assistant and she's looking to hire another vet. She was able to take her first vacation in years — to the Caribbean. And I told her to turn her phone *off*. When she returned, her business was just as healthy as it was when she left, because she learned how to build relationships.

Another vet client of mine was experiencing the same problem. Her business was out of control because it was growing so fast. Again, she was the worker bee of the business, and she didn't know which way to go. She knew she needed help. At that time, she only had one office assistant. Eventually, she hired an assistant in the truck and three more staff. She learned to standardize the experience given by her new bees, and as the Super Bee, saw the hive grow far more productively.

Both of these women have great personalities, they're hard workers, but they weren't doing the daunting work of planning and taking certain actions for the business. They both realized that this was something that they had to face if they wanted growth.

Doing the Difficult Work

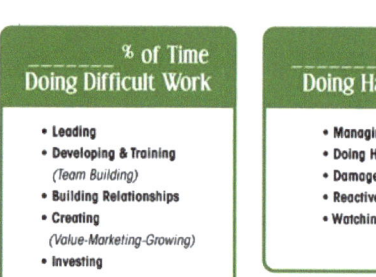

_____ % of Time
Doing Difficult Work

- Leading
- Developing & Training
  (Team Building)
- Building Relationships
- Creating
  (Value-Marketing-Growing)
- Investing

_____ % of Time
Doing Hard Work

- Managing
- Doing Hard Work
- Damage Control
- Reactive Work
- Watching Expenses

To see a transformation in your business, you need to set it up today the way you want it to be. It's about being on purpose. A lot of people today avoid the reason why they are in business. They look at it as self-employment and feel that as long as they work hard, they are doing okay. If you want to achieve work-life balance, you have to start focusing on the business side.

Chapter 3 — Strategic Turning Point

$$* * *$$

"The best time to plant a tree was 20 years ago.
The second best time is now." —Chinese Proverb

In every business, you come to a point when you've hit a ceiling and you just can't take that business any higher. For us, our pharmacy was doing okay — we were actually doing better than most businesses — but it wasn't good enough. It wasn't giving us the results that we wanted. I also did not like the path that the industry was taking, because we were all becoming the same.

Every business was discounting their front-end products and trying to get customers to come in and get their prescriptions filled. As you would you expect, our margins kept shrinking and shrinking. We were making our distributors happy, but we weren't happy ourselves.

I wanted to transform it into a business working for us *instead of* us working in the business all the time. I came up with a strategic turning point and I've never looked back.

I began to realize that there were three things that I wanted to accomplish. First, I wanted to repackage our business. Second, I needed to deliver more value to my customers so that in return I would get more value back. Third, I wanted to increase the number of visits or the size of the shopping cart when they came in. I wanted them to spend more money with us, and for us to be able to satisfy more of their wants.

As business owners, we are on one side of a mountain. We all want to get to the top, because there's something there that we want to have.

Climbing Mountains

Now, across the valley, there's a larger mountain. That mountain represents other people, the consumers and the customers. Each one wants to climb the mountain, just like you, for their own reasons. In the veterinary business, customers who climb that mountain are concerned about their pets, their horses, their cattle, etc. However, it is still a commercial product and a service, and the way you are going to give it to them is in your hands.

How? By building a bridge between your mountain and theirs. That bridge is your business. Not a profession, because you already have a profession. This was a strategic turning point for me, when I figured out that the business side needed more of my attention, and the business was just the bridge that brought our professional services to the masses.

Working on Purpose

Around twenty years ago, we decided to quit selling tobacco products, even though they were a pretty good profit-turner for our pharmacy. And I was "on purpose" when I said, "Why are we selling tobacco, which is harmful for your health, in the front end, and selling products that help quit smoking in the back end?"

I knew then that selling tobacco was not in our mission statement. We therefore became the first pharmacy to get out of selling cigarettes. We took a hit in our sales and profits, but we went on purpose, trusting that it was the right thing to do. Because of our intent, we won the prestigious Barb Tarbox award, for being the first pharmacy to stop selling cigarettes before it was law.

My daughter Ayn, now a registered nurse, and me, receiving the Barb Tarbox Award of Excellence

As a veterinarian, there might be some practices that are common in the industry that you might want to change or remove from your business. It is important that you stay true to your mission and the statement that you want to make. Some practitioners, for example, are being forced to push products to their customers. You don't want to be a salesperson in that manner. You want to be in a position where you suggest some items and are of assistance in terms of what's going to be best for that patient. We wanted to position ourselves as a true health provider, and to create a culture around this position as a healthy living store. We sacrificed money to do the right thing, but ended up with a lot of free advertising from it, not to mention national exposure. (I've included the write-up at the end of the book.) And we kept our customers because we were building a relationship, a bridge between our wants and theirs.

Having the courage to trust your gut instincts is a big factor in discovering your own strategic turning points.

Some time ago, I was going to a seminar in Vegas. Back home, we had a new baby, a toddler and a brand new store. I was wondering why I was even going to the seminar! I opened my briefcase to pull out my book to read. It had a note in it that Lorraine had written. She must have known that I didn't really know if I wanted to go, because she had written, "We go for a reason and sometimes we don't know what that reason is."

When I got to the seminar, there were only twelve participants and there were seven speakers. One of them was Dan Kennedy. Another one was Alan Jacks. They are big names in business and marketing, and I got to rub shoulders with them during that weekend. I've been to some of the speakers' homes, and some of the participants' homes — top real estate investment leaders in Canada — and to this day, I can pick up the phone and talk to them if I want to. Even though I didn't know my purpose at first, I made sure that I followed up with them after the seminar and I expanded my network.

With the support of Lorraine, I trusted my instinct that going to this seminar would be important for our business, and was rewarded by the incredible knowledge and relationships I was able to gain and build there.

Chapter 4 — Productivity Levers: Equity and Energy

* * *

"The person who says it cannot be done should not interrupt the person who is doing it." —Chinese Proverb

In Chapter 1, we talked about the disconnect between your profession and your business, and how important it is to diagnose the difference. This understanding is the beginning of your own Transformational Experience, which we discussed in Chapter 2. Chapter 3 introduced you to the idea of the Strategic Turning Point — building a bridge to link you and your goals with your customers and theirs. In this chapter we're going to step it up, challenging you to be courageous as we delve deeper into our diagnosis.

How efficient are you? How are you getting things done? Do you wonder if the time and energy you spend are really translating into reasonable equity and assets? Maximizing these two Productivity Levers, your return-on-energy and your return-on-equity, (your REs) will in turn change everything about the return you see in your business.

So, again, what we do now is analyze. We go in and diagnose: how you spend your energy and how you spend your assets, or your equity.

How do you leverage your energy? If you're working in your profession all day, is there some part in that day that you can delegate to someone else? This someone can do certain lower-level tasks, at a lesser equity cost to you, freeing up your own time, so you can then become more productive with other things in your day and get more of the higher-level things done. This is the great advantage of delegating — having everyone on your team, including you, working at the highest of their potential. Harness their strengths, to better be able to utilize your own.

So what we're going to try to do is work with your strength. And your strength is your profession. There are no two ways about it. You've worked really hard to be in your profession and to get that veterinary license. That's your energy's best bet. But at the same time, you can leverage the equity of others or the equity of your cash flow and make those work for you. The main goal is you want to become an asset CEO. This means now you're always managing your return-on-equity and your return-on-energy, but you're making sure that you pay yourself first — either with time off or with income.

An example of leveraging your return-on-equity as an asset CEO would be, for example, buying a vaccine from a Boehringer Igelheim. You purchase the vaccine and you on-sell it to one of your patients at a healthy mark-up (if you can!) Obviously, the bigger the mark-up (by offering a premium product) or the bigger the volume of vaccines you sell — the higher your return-on-equity.

"I'm sorry, does that say $777? It should be $111. I mistakenly calculated your bill in dog dollars."

An example of leveraging your return-on-energy would be implementing a system for hiring new staff that you create and set up one time — but that your staff can implement for you without your involvement (except perhaps at the end, to interview the most-qualified candidates).

If you can leverage these two assets, and be constantly aware of improving them, you can compound the results, and you can become far more effective, making your business that much stronger.

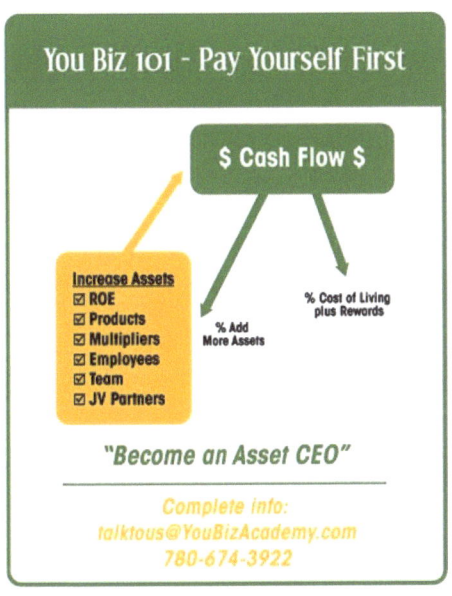

In my experience, the most effective way to boost your efficiency is to identify the things that you do really well, and bring those skills or systems to an even higher level. When you own a business, it's natural that you manage a lot of things, and you ask your employees to finish many tasks for you. However, what happens then is you lower your efficiency. Instead of doing ten tasks at 100% efficiency, you end up doing twenty or more things at only 5% efficiency. So, evaluate your business and look at the things that you have been doing all this time, and where you'd like to be with them. Choose just a few points to start, and keep evaluating until you perfect them. You should be really clear on where you want to go, or you will never know how you're going to get there.

I applied this principle when I was coaching hockey. What my team needed to do was move up the ice, from one end to the other, to score a goal — the desired result — which is not an easy feat considering that there are six angry opponents heading straight for you, determined to interrupt your progress. So I broke the process down into smaller pieces, and then broke these down even further. I divided the ice into three zones: the first goal line to the first blue line, the blue line to the next blue line, and then that blue line to the next goal line. And in between those zones I created baby steps.

We ended up initiating two breakouts, two middle zone plays, and two offensive zone plays. It brought us great success because we became very efficient at the things that we were already good at. We became very repetitive. We improved the play, making it better and better each time.

I then applied the same principle to our store. I challenged myself to double our profit and effectiveness one year. I selected the seven biggest things in our business that would help our profitability and productivity. And then I really compounded it by focusing our efforts on what I call the "multipliers" in our business: people and technology.

I kept this focus for three years, and each year we doubled our profit.

After the third year, we kept making improvements to our processes to increase revenue and stay ahead of our competitors. I know that you can double the profit and productivity of your business as I did, using this same strategy, because I've proven it works with veterinary practices as well as our own pharmacy.

Chapter 5 — Igniting Your Third Factor

* * *

"There are no traffic jams along the extra mile." —Roger
Staubach

This next topic that I want to take up is the real key to
making that shift from being just a business owner to
being a true entrepreneur. And this is what I call
igniting your Third Factor. I believe that this is the most
important concept for you to understand, because it is the
thing that will differentiate you from the rest of the
marketplace. It will also give you the most leverage and
return on your investment.

Let me break the concept down into three things: product,
service and the Third Factor.

Product

When you start a business, you offer a product to the market
— and that product happens to be your profession. You
want to offer the best product, so you undergo training and
take up additional education to be the best you can be in the

profession. But having the best product can only take you so far. Consumers want something more than just the product.

Service

So what you do is analyze your profession, and you try to discover ways in which you can leverage it. This is where service comes in. We want to provide faster delivery of our expertise, so we bring in more people to the organization. We want to provide a better user experience, so we introduce customer support. We want to meet the expectations of our customers by giving them what they need. Added service gives added value and better opportunity for clients to deal with us.

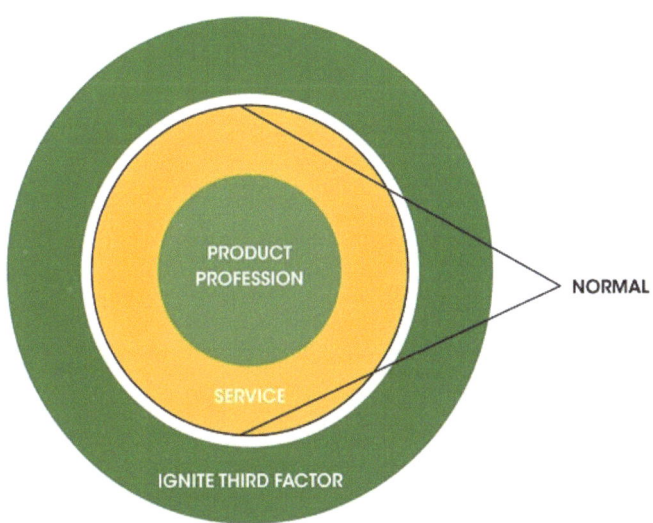

Doing the Difficult Work

PRODUCT
PROFESSION

NORMAL

SERVICE

IGNITE THIRD FACTOR

The Third Factor

After product and service, people still want more. What do you do next? This is where we move to the most important part, igniting your Third Factor. This is the big differential and the game changer. This is the portion where you want your customers to have a better day because they came in contact with your organization. You want them to have a better experience with you than they would have with your competitors.

Picture yourself on a regular day on your way to gas up your car. You can simply go down a gasoline alley and pick a Shell, a Petro Canada or a Chevron station. All three can give the same product and the same service, so it doesn't matter which one you choose. On a certain day you will go to Shell, and the next you can go to Chevron, and you won't feel bad about it, but you won't feel good about it either. You don't wish for your customers to be in this same situation.

You have to think really hard on how you can make your business the top choice. Position yourself as the number one place to go, by giving something a little bit different than everyone else. You can get suggestions from your employees or ask your existing customers. Or you can join a group with fellow vets to discuss how you can all improve your practices or your businesses.

Igniting your Third Factor is the differentiator. You make the strategy of moving from simply providing a product and a service, because it is commonplace, it makes you just another one of the players. Why do you think people are willing to spend for an expensive coffee in Starbucks? True, they have good quality coffee, but it's the experience they give of *a coffee shop that seems like a home.*

Paving the Way to
Increased Prosperity and a Life-Balance

In igniting your Third Factor, there are what we call the Three Levers of Advantage. They are: leadership, creativity and relationships.

Leadership is about having vision and direction, which is why it's important to take time to think about your business. It's about maximizing your strengths, minimizing dangers and focusing on opportunities.

I like to use an analogy about the difference in the roles of dogs that pull sleds. How do the leaders get picked? How about the swing or point dogs, which is the second group of dogs? Then you have the team dogs, the wheel dogs. Each one has a purpose. It's all about personality. After owning them for so many years, you can tell by their personality what that dog will do.

My first experience racing in a mass start, a very exhilarating experience

Wheel dogs are the ones that are directly in front of the sled. They are muscle dogs, because they are usually the strongest and the most fearless. Team dogs are just happy to be running with everybody else. The point dog is the cheerleader, or the energy dog that cheers the leader dog. The leader dog does all the thinking. There's a lot of pressure on the lead dog, because there's a whole team that's relying on that one dog.

It is tough being a leader, you and I both know it, and the burnout rate is fast. As the musher, or the man leading the sled, you cannot steer the dogs, but you can encourage them to do the right thing. And they need a trail to run on. Well, in this example you're not the lead dog, you're the musher or the conductor. You encourage your employees and even your customers towards the right direction, to bring out the best in them. They trust you to make the right decisions on the trail.

Lead dogs Diva and Crackers

Creativity involves thinking of different ways to get results by introducing small changes to your systems and processes. It's about resourcefulness, working with what you have, and turning that around to your advantage. It also requires certain problem-solving skills, experimenting through trial and error, knowledge and talent.

The last lever is building *relationships*. When you have a solid relationship with your clients, you also build trust and confidence. They will keep coming back to you because they know your capacity and that you care about them. It's the same way with your employees. When you build and maintain relationships, you build loyalty. And loyalty is priceless when it comes to business. Also, expand your network and build relationships with people in the same field as you or with other people who are also in business for themselves. You never know the kind of insights that you will get.

Three Levers of Advantage

Build your business around the concept of adding value. Igniting your Third Factor is building around what you believe and what your customers believe. You can't afford to have a disconnect between the services that you offer and what your customers expect. You can make your business stand out from everybody else because you've created a relationship with your customers that's so strong, they can't live without you.

Our VIP logo — by far our biggest-winning marketing undertaking

This concept of adding value is the driving force behind our Smart Shopper Club, an absolute Third Factor winner for us and our premier clients, positioned so our customers never feel like they are being sold. It's a done-for-you system of rewarding our best clients — a business plan to retain customers, to create a flood of traffic on demand and to leverage for ourselves an owner's return on equity and energy. This kind of program is an absolute MUST strategy for anyone with a professional business.

Your business model needs to deliver awareness that your business is an investment like any other investment. In these modern times, you need to have a change of mindset. The vet practice ten years ago was different from the way it is today. In short, create a position statement for you as the owner, for the consumer, and for your employees, too.

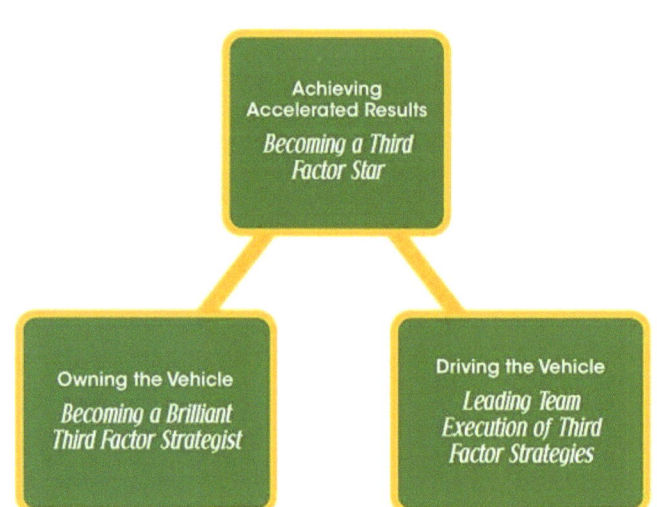

Chapter 6 — The Six Most Costly Mistakes: Lessons Learned from Being in the Trenches

* * *

"Every strike brings me closer to the next home run." —Babe Ruth

N ow that we've discussed the steps you need to take to transform yourself and your business, I want to let you in on the mistakes that I've made in the past. These mistakes have cost me a lot — use them as cautionary tales! At some point in your business, you're going to make mistakes, or perhaps you feel you already have. When I look back, I wish I had known these things before I made these mistakes. But made them I did, and they were lessons I learned the hard way. I am going to share them with you so you can avoid them earlier on in your business.

1. Not treating your business as an investment (of equity and energy).

A lot of business owners think that when they own a business, they will no longer have time for themselves. This mistake of accepting that you have no control over what happens to your business takes away your freedom. Instead, you could have the life that you want, even while you are running your business today.

Another mistake is thinking that you can only get that freedom after you sell your business. Instead, you should love your business now, while you are still building it, and continually strive to have it work for you. By improving your processes one step at a time, you will get closer to attaining a lifestyle by choice, not a lifestyle by chance. Don't wait until you sell your business to enjoy the money that it made, and don't let your business suck your life away. You can gain cash flow and wealth and you can enjoy it *today*.

2. Falling into the commodity trap.

The movie *Avatar* was a great success. It won nine Academy Awards and scored big in the box office, even surpassing *Titanic*. Yet critics think that, aside from the amazing special effects, the storyline is forgettable (unlike its counterparts, *Star Wars* and *Lord of the Rings*). For them, it's what they call a classic Hollywood commodity trap. Why? Because the script seemed like it was taken from a lot of past movies, and it wasn't different enough.

As a business owner, the very last thing you want your clients to feel is that your services are replaceable with those of any other veterinary practice. I have used many vets over the years to treat our animals on the farm — the vast majority I couldn't recall even if I'd wanted to. Why? Because there was nothing remarkable about them. Nothing different that set them apart and made them stand out from the crowd. I say that with one exception. Our current vet is marvellous. The best vet I have ever worked with. She is highly knowledgeable, extremely responsive and one of the nicest people you could ever hope to meet. She won't run tests unless she thinks they're absolutely necessary. She calls back about test results (instead of telling us to call), and she'll call up the day after visiting our sick animals to check on their progress. This woman is a diamond in in these parts. I heard of another vet who, after putting a horse to sleep, would embroider a bookmark using the horse's tail, in the Navajo tradition — to give to the grieving owner. In the owner's eyes, there is no other vet who could replace her care and attention. That's another way of Igniting Your Third Factor — setting yourself apart from your competition.

The bottom line is this — if you run your business just the same as all the other vets, it's going to be very hard for clients to tell your services apart from your competitors', and that's when people start looking at the only remaining factor, price, and start shopping around for vets who offer the cheapest prices — which is a situation you *never* want to be in.

Customers lining up to come to our store — despite the blizzard conditions!

3. Busy beehive syndrome.

It's easy to be busy. But the question is, does this bring results? Are you running a business, or a *busy*-ness? Since you started out as a professional, you probably got used to doing everything by yourself. You have this habit of being the worker bee and not positioning yourself as the leader, the Super Bee.

One thing that you may not be paying enough attention to is scheduling strategic planning time. Another habit that you should get rid of is driving your vehicle (business) pedal-to-the-metal, with no destination in mind (lifestyle by chance, not choice). Another thing to aim for is getting in the habit of leveraging the return-on-equity and return-on-energy in every business decision. And last, make sure you are multiplying yourself by using the strength of others.

4. Chasing too many chickens.

I mentioned this in the previous chapter. Doing a thousand things poorly, or chasing too many chickens, or will only lead to distraction and lack of focus. Instead, focus on only four to seven critical success factors and structuring systems. And then make sure these core things are attended to and being done really, really well. These critical success factors are closely related to the mission and vision of your business. Some examples would include: increasing competitiveness by faster delivery of products, sustaining successful relationship with suppliers and retaining staff with customer-focused training.

5. Not unleashing your unlimited potential.

There's power in becoming an asset CEO within your organization. This is why you need to spend more time thinking about your business rather than doing all the hard work. You also need to expand your thinking and explore what the future for your business could look like. Once you unleash your unlimited potential, you will be able to leverage your REs, make things happen with the magic of systems, and gain multiple streams of income.

6. As owners, we don't get out of our own way.

So you own your own business — big deal. The last of the costly mistakes that you could make is that you set such high standards for yourself that you accept the fact that you can't be replaced. The result? You still end up doing everything. You should change your mindset and apply the 80/20 rule throughout your organization. This means that you should hire the best talent for your company if you want good results.

As a benchmark, someone who is 60–80% as good as you is usually good enough in a well-run, system-driven company. Other successful companies even hire people who are better than they are. If you have quality employees, then you can expect quality results. Use the unique abilities of others in the right areas of your business to bring your company to higher standards than if you only did the work yourself.

Another application of the 80/20 rule is finding your best buyers — 80% of your revenue is represented by 20% of your customers. In fact, you can even go deeper by looking for the top 20% from the 20%. Once you figure out who your best buyers are, your company should adapt towards meeting the needs of these customers.

Another trap that you could fall into is spending your own time to save money. Because you think about your limited budget, you tend to not hire people or not spend on equipment or software that would speed up processes. Since you are not investing in these things, your business will never get ahead, as you keep on trying to catch up with delays.

Our coaching program comes with a delegation filtering system that can significantly improve the performance of your organization.

Chapter 7 — The Magic of Making Things Happen

$* * *$

"Winning isn't everything, but wanting to win is." —Vince Lombardi

If you have learned a lot from the previous chapters, this is where it all comes together. All the principles and concepts of growing your business come down to this: making things happen. I'd like to share with you this quote from Michael Jordan, "Some people want it to happen, some wish it would happen, others make it happen." As a professional and a business owner, you can *want* to make things happen — or you can choose to really *make* things happen.

In my coaching group, I ask if any of them have bought any kind of fitness equipment. Many raise their hands. When I ask how many of them use the fitness equipment as a clothes hanger, everybody laughs. It's funny because it's true. The buying part is easy, but using it to exercise and get fit is harder, and people often just give up. Successful people dream, plan and envision their goals just like everyone else.

What makes the difference? You're right. They act on their plans each day to get what they want.

The magic of making things happen is using small hinges to open big doors. As I said earlier, the answer does not lie in drastic and gigantic measures. The answer is in the little things, looking at what it is that you can change in order to get results. It's really not that different from joining a fitness program. At the beginning, it's difficult to get up early and hit the gym. Yet as you get along, you become stronger and stronger because you have that goal of becoming healthy and having a good body.

"Word to the wise: Always check the cheese for pills."

The most organized people get closest to their goals. This is because they remove the clutter, the unnecessary distractions, and get clear on the path that they want to take. That is when the magic starts to happen. Compound on the little things that you are doing right, and then transform those into even bigger players for you.

Let me give you another example. Chasing your goal is like chasing a bunch of chickens. You don't step into the chicken coop and just try to grab as many chickens as you can in one go. Instead, you try to catch one chicken at a time until you get all the chickens that you want.

In the first year of our coaching program, we help those who join the program to take just nine impact areas that would help them double their business. We don't do an overload by chasing 100 things. Choose nine impact areas and you will definitely transform your business and achieve greater results. If you're unsure of what those areas are, we are here to help you. With my twenty-eight years of experience in business, we can drill down to the nine most effective things that will leverage your time and assets to make your veterinary practice a better business for you. Then from this point forward, all you need is to embrace the change that is coming to your company, keep moving, maintain a positive attitude, and never quit.

"Do not give up. Beginning is always the hardest."
—Unknown

Conclusion

* * *

"You miss 100% of the shots you don't take" —Wayne Gretzky

Let me tell you one last story about how I've gotten to this point in my life. How I moved beyond running a pharmacy, to unleash my own potential as a true entrepreneur, and used my new knowledge and skills not only back at my original business, but in countless new opportunities.

A friend of mine came over to our house one day and told me about a real estate investing course that he had taken. Apparently he was doing quite well with it, and asked me if I'd like to join him. At that time, our pharmacy was doing okay. I was managing it as usual, and I thought that it was somewhat in the stable state that I wanted it to be in. So, I thought that it might just be time for me to look into investing in other businesses, so that we were not putting all our eggs in one basket.

I said "Yes" to my friend and paid $900 to go to the seminar. It was a package that included a one-day course about how to invest in real estate. Even now, $900 is not an easy amount to just throw around, and its value was much higher back then. We certainly didn't have it just lying around, because our kids were still young, and we had invested a lot of money in the pharmacy. Still, I went with my friend because I was intrigued by the things that he was telling us and the potential that it presented.

I attended the seminar and learned much that I implemented in our business. It was an unforgettable experience. It gave me an education and I learned how to drive our business in the direction that I wanted. These are things that I learned outside of my industry and it made me look at the business world a whole lot differently. The pharmacy industry was also at a critical stage, and these new insights really helped me.

The seminar was full of valuable information. It taught me how to run multiple businesses. When you reach the level of running many businesses, you need to step out of the frontline and out of the hands-on managing of the operations of the business. I also discovered the importance and the compounding effect of continuing education.

I saw that there was a lot more to gain, which is why I decided to take the orientation course. Afterwards, we made that extra stretch and we started investing in real estate. We had a very aggressive goal of buying one property every six months, so we would have two properties a year. This experience of investing is still part of the learning process, because we learned how to deal with people and with banks.

There were around forty of us in that orientation course, and we were all having trouble getting our real estate businesses to another level. It was kind of a strategic turning point for us. We started our own focus group, all forty of us. We decided to meet each month, each shelling out five dollars to cover the room charge.

It was the first time I had experienced and witnessed the true power of gathering with a group of like-minded people from the same industry, who were also very aggressive in their thinking.

A day sportfishing with colleagues and other pharmacy owners — caught and released this nice sail fish — an adrenaline rush!

We discovered from our discussions that the things that were stopping us were the same things that were stopping our business. We also figured out some strategies about marketing, how to position our businesses into something that was different than everyone else, and how to value the people that we were paying to help build our portfolio. We shifted our focus to buying properties for tenants, not for ourselves. I applied the same shift of focus to our business. We put the spotlight on the customer and studied how we could make their day and their experience better when they came to our pharmacy.

For me, getting around a group of people with the same goal unleashed many opportunities, not only in our real estate investments, but also in the business that we already had.

I believe doing the same thing will also help you and your business.

Our learning programs are composed of three levels: the Inner Circle, the Premier Coaching Program, and the Master's Program.

The Inner Circle is where you'll get started, as I did, by having a gathering, or what we call a "Mastermind" session, with professionals and business owners that are in the same stage as you are. This group meeting happens over the phone once a month for thirty to forty-five minutes. It is also a mentorship program where you will have the chance to have a one-on-one discussion with a proven business coach. You will also receive one email communication per week or four emails per month.

There is a three-month minimum term, because I believe it is in repetition that you start to see results. Each Mastermind group will have a maximum of ten members. Once you sign up, you will be put on a waiting list and the program will start when the target number of members has been reached. Should you find that you are too advanced for this level, we can accelerate you to the Premier Coaching or the Master's Program, depending on your level.

Premier Coaching, the second level of my program, includes everything that is in the Inner Circle program, plus one hour a month of live, one-on-one coaching with me. You also get two emails per week instead of one.

The third level is the Master's Program. You will get everything in Premier Coaching, but now you get a weekly one-on-one coaching with me, to firmly put you in the driver's seat of your practice. Our email communications are unlimited. The biggest bonus at this level is that you will have a total strategic plan that will analyze your entire business. This process involves a lot of evaluation and questions and answers, until we can design the perfect marketing plan for your business. This program is backed with a robust guarantee. You commit to the Master's Program for one year, and if after implementing all my recommendations I have not been able to double your results, I will refund your entire year's coaching fee.

You're probably overwhelmed or excited about the great opportunities that might come your way. There is only one thing you need to do to get started: visit our website, YouBiz Academy.com, and schedule a free fifteen minute discovery and strategy session with me. You can get a lot of advice in just fifteen minutes, and you get it for free.

Here are some of the things that my vet clients have said about the program:

"After the first meeting, the concepts that you were presenting to me were not like anything I had done before, so I very much wanted to come out of there with more, and I felt really energized after our first meeting. I felt like the subsequent follow-ups on the phone would be really helpful... My confidence, I think, is the thing I've seen the biggest difference in as an owner. I feel way more confident knowing where I need to work from a business standpoint, and just knowing where to draw the line in recognizing who I want to retain as a client and who I want to let go. I feel way more confident in making that kind of decision."
— Dr. Miranda, owned practice since March 2013

"I walked away feeling optimistic that the direction we were going and this process was going to ultimately lead to a more successful business and I left feeling that I had gained more business education — it was nice to learn something new and how to approach veterinarian business as opposed to just veterinarian medicine... I always enjoy hearing how other veterinarians are doing and how they approach things and how we have all faced very similar struggles and it's just nice to share the experiences and support each other. It's nice that the group is so supportive of each other..."
— Dr. Danica, owned practice since 2012

Do you want to be able to have that dream vacation soon? Are you looking forward to having the freedom and flexibility to achieve that work-life balance that you've wanted for years? If so, then schedule your free consultation with me today by visiting our website at YouBizAcademy.com, and fill out a contact form.

An adventure holiday — a drift dive (Lorraine's first!) off Maui Crater

Whether you choose to participate in the coaching programs we offer, or in another program, or even just to informally get together with your own group of like-minded, positive people to share ideas with and support each other as you elevate your own enterprises to the next level — always keep moving upwards through your ceilings. Leveraging yourself and your potential as you navigate the challenges we all face takes courage and the fortitude to do the hard work of critically analyzing your own strengths. Working smarter, not harder, will reward that courage with greater returns of growth in both your profession and your business. Remember, you are your own best asset!

Barb Tarbox Award of Excellence

* * *